Dear Terror

by
Christopher Bursk

Published by

**Read
Furiously**

Read Often. Read Well.

Published by Read Furiously. First Edition.

ISBN: 978-1-7337360-4-6

Poetry
Poetry Collection – Single Author

For more information on *Dear Terror* or Read Furiously, please visit readfuriously.com. For inquiries, please contact samantha@readfuriously.com.

Cover Artwork by Danielle Bursk
Interior Artwork by Danielle Bursk
Cover Layout by Adam Wilson
Layout by Adam Wilson

Edited by Samantha Atzeni

Read (v): The act of interpreting and understanding the written word.

Furiously (adv): To engage in an activity with passion and excitement.

**Read Often. Read Well.
Read Furiously**

For Bernadette Karpa, Jo Freehand, Carly Volpe
my *Read Furiously* compatriots
who have taught me what courage is

For poets Phyllis Purscell, Luray Gross, Hayden Saunier
        Lynn Levin, and Marie Kane
who have taught me what grace is

For the community of poets of Bucks County
who have taught me what valor is

For my family who keep trying to teach me
what joy is
&
In memory of Rick Churchill, Sandy Becker, David Kime,
who teach me new lessons every day

Table of Contents

Dear Terror,

Old mentor, brother–in–arms,
most loyal companion
in the operating room and holding cell,
at the cliff with no railing or the creaking ice,
down the long hallway leading who knows where,
on the empty stairwell, the wrong side
of the door, my father's deathbed,
crib of my newborn grandchild,
don't worry.
I won't forsake you.

Sisters

I understood I could no more call them to me
than I could make my mother let go of my brother's throat,
or summon my father back from the world
he, like Odysseus, preferred to us,
and yet, on the very nights I vowed not to need anyone
ever again, the sisters returned,

all six with the same silver eyes,
the same long hair the color of steel
that'd been rained on
for weeks, the same stoop to the shoulders
all six looking exactly alike, though I could always tell
each from the other:

the one so hurt she smiles all the time;
the one so happy she looks away
when anyone turns to her; the mute sister;
the sister who speaks for them all;
the sister with no hope;
the sister with enough hope for them all.

One played with my ear, the way my mother used to,
before she decided to kill me.
One twirled strands of my hair around her finger,
so tight to my scalp she must've known
how much I counted on that hurt;
one tested the wings of my back; one rubbed my belly

till every part of me fell obediently asleep
but my eyes. The mute sister kissed my eyelids
closed. The one with hope for all of us sang
and sang the way a brook might
make music with the most ordinary of things – leaf, stick –
and then they'd all join in.

They have sung to me for more years
than I've a right to wish for,
sang when my children were out of sorts
or I was washing my father's darkest secrets
from his buttocks, or opening a letter
that said what I feared it would say,

or when the police seized me
by the ankles on the day that madman ascended the throne
of the world and threatened
to crush it between his thumb and forefinger,
and though, just last night
in my dreams I stirred to their voices as old as water's

conversation with the stones,
all six sisters singing as one,
even the mute one mouthing with such vibrato
she seemed to be bellowing,
and though I've listened to this song
since I grew old enough to feel guilty

for all I had done and could not do,
and though, waking, I've tried to pull the verses back
out of the dry, locked places
of my mind, I cannot make any music pulse
in my throat. I'd do almost anything to be able to sing
with my sisters, sing right now their words

　　　　to you.

In the Second Year of the Presidency

Every day Tyler visits his Opa
his Opa makes sure
there's a forest fire
only Tyler can put out
or a flood
only Tyler can stop in its path,
Then Tyler turns thirteen
and his Opa watches from the window
as the boy shoots hoops
by himself. Sometimes
the ball doesn't bother
with the rim. It nestles in the net.
The net welcomes it,
then immediately lets it go.
Sends it on its way.
No strings attached.
For a moment
Tyler's Opa forgets the planet is doomed.

Are You a Friend of Dorothy's?

"But – see here!" said Jack Pumpkinhead with a gasp. "If you become a girl, you won't be my dear father anymore!"

"No," answered Tip laughing, in spite of his anxiety. "And I shall not be sorry to escape the relationship," though he added hesitatingly as he turned to Glinda, "I might try for a while just to see how it seems, you know. But if I don't like being a girl you must promise to change me back into a boy again."

There were only a few places in town where a boy was free
to be a girl and Juvenile Fiction

in the Paul Pratt Memorial Library was one
and the other was my mother's full-length mirror

where, with no one home,
I could be as naked as glass and cross my legs

so tightly you'd never guess
I ever was a boy.

There Was Something
Seriously Wrong

1

There was something seriously wrong
with me. I knew it. You knew it.
The girl whom I'd just rolled off
knew it. I never told anyone
about you. Not even the men my father paid
to make me well. I made myself
believe you never existed. I practiced
putting a tender part of me
into a tender part of someone else. I even fell
in love with her. We had children
I loved so much
I didn't think I had a right
to love anyone else. Who are you
to say otherwise,
to push your way back into my life?
Who are you to put words in my mouth?

2

You've written nothing of worth
on your own. You ought to know by now
every word is a collaboration.
You owe me more
than can ever be repaid.
I don't ask for much.
At least give me a name.

At Night I Don't Have to Say Anything

He's there even before I know I need him.
Sometimes he's a child

who's just wrestled himself free from a wave.
Sometimes he's a teenager

trying to convince himself he likes the taste of beer.
Sometimes he's a boy from the football team

I quit, fifty years ago
leaving shoulder, hip, and knee pads neatly on the 20-yard line.

Sometimes he has a name – Esteban, Theo, D. B.
Sometimes he doesn't.

Sometimes he takes off my shirt, button by button.
Sometimes I rip his off.

Shhh, he says, as I sob into the little hollow
between his shoulder and neck.

Certain days I feel America under my feet
turning into quicksand.

Certain days I can't speak
because every word turns into rotting fruit

as soon as I bite into it.
I have a wife who for some reason is not repulsed

by me, and children who'd forgive me
almost everything, but certain nights

I need someone whose life I can't possibly ruin,
someone a god might have wanted

so much he had to turn him into a flower
or a branch

that'd spring back as soon as you let go of it,
and he's there at my side –

Simeon, Ezra, Praktish, Alayne, Rafe?
Who am I to refuse him?

Delivering the Famous Poet to His Hotel

Do I have someone in my life I worry about?
Do I hate the feeling of snow under my collar?
Have I ever tried to walk on water?
What song do I sing to my infant grandson

as I rub his belly
and watch his eyes decide whether or not to flutter shut?

Famous poet, before you take a nap
while I wait in the lobby for you to be done dreaming
ask me just one question.
That'd be enough.

As a boy I used to collect feathers.
I thought if I saved enough, I'd put together a whole bird.
I was seven. I still thought it possible
for a boy like me to fly.

If It's Not His Fault, Then Whose Is It?

Not his father's
His father had more important things to do
than come all the way home
just to put out a small fire.

Not his mother's.
It was her job to hold the boy's hand
close to the fire so he finally understood
just how hungry it might be.

Don't blame his brothers
for making fun of the bears,
those droopy old souls
his mother commanded the boy set on fire.

Was it the bears' fault
they were so soft
the boy had undressed
and held them next to his bare skin?

Can he hold the flames accountable
for doing what they've been created to do:
never to leave the table
without finishing their supper?

Amnesty Helmet™

Sooner than you think, you won't need your mouth

to talk

you into forgiving yourself for what

you know

you don't deserve forgiveness. In the future

there'll be a helmet

specifically designed to read your thoughts and

redeem you.

Gone will be the need to hoard shame

convinced

you've at least one thing no one could take from you:

how you'd failed

your father and then your son, griefs you cling to

like shipwreck.

Now all you'll need to do is accept the helmet

offered,

let it persuade every cell in your brain

to be pardoned

Once everything's forgiven

by electricity,

you won't even require a mouth

to swallow,

back words, the magnanimous electrodes willing

to do the hard work

the mind had to before, the heart was never

quite up to.

Soon serenity will be strapped to your chin.

Soon

there'll be no un—re—programmable guilt, no longing

a logarithm

can't mitigate, no rancor it won't withstand,

a right voltage

even for those of you who, wanting to hurt

no one

brought so much hurt to those you loved.

Even you

can be interceded for! Soon there'll be an

amnesty

you can slide over your ears and buckle. Once

there's hope

for you, what, pray tell, what will you do

with that suddenly

emptied mind, a mouth that still yearns

to confess:

there must be something terrible it can still admit,

a nakedness safe

from electricity's relentless search party,

time's bright angel?

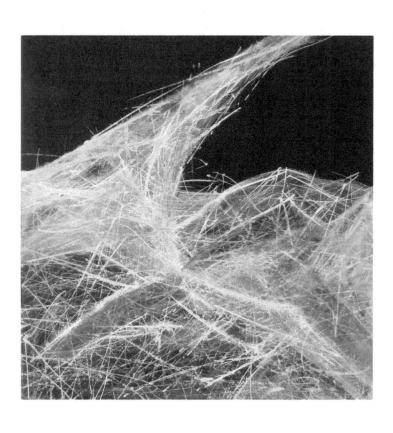

The First Day of School

I'd never seen so many children

                    my age

          in one place, some

with bright hair,

               some

        with furrowed brows,

One even had freckles darting

                  under his collar.

        My fingers needed

to know if he was speckled

                down to his toes.

        I wanted to run up and touch

everyone in kindergarten

              to see if he

        or she was real.

slip my hand inside a shirt,

                search for nipples

        like mine,

a belly button? Innie

                or outie?

        Perhaps it's lucky

I realized then

                  going up to another child

        and stroking his face

might not be a good idea.

              I didn't

        even open my mouth.

Let my tongue give in

              to the pleasures

        of vowels

and consonants? Then wouldn't

              the hands

        demand to do

what all day they'd itched to do?

              And then

        there'd be no stopping me.

The Knife

The snow's waist high
but the three men on my closet door
wade into the little valley
winter has made between my house
and everyone else's.
as if a blizzard can no more stop them
than the sea could discourage men determined
to swim to its horizon. And then
right before my eyes
two of the men grab the third
and hold him so tight
it looks as if they're trying to warm him with their bodies,
but soon his coat's off,
they must have pulled it over his head
along with his shirt,
and I don't know why they want him stripped
to his skin on this night
of all nights, and though there's no moon
I see there's a knife.
as clearly as if it's been lifted over my head
as over that trembling man with his bare, soft belly.
He's being held
from behind — the way I've seen my father sometimes
seize hold of my mother.
Jewels glitter on the knife handle.
The man wielding it
is smiling, but his is not a cruel mouth.
It's the smile of a someone who knows he has no choice
but to do what he must do.
And then on the closet door:
blood. I hadn't expected it to be this red
I throw off my bedcovers,
I pad on bare feet across the floor.
And now I can smell blood
on my hands. See?

Does Your Father Suspect

Does your father realize
you are not his child?
Did your mother suspect
what she'd been carrying in her womb?
You looked human
enough
but there must have been a reason
she set you on a neighbor's porch
and walked away.

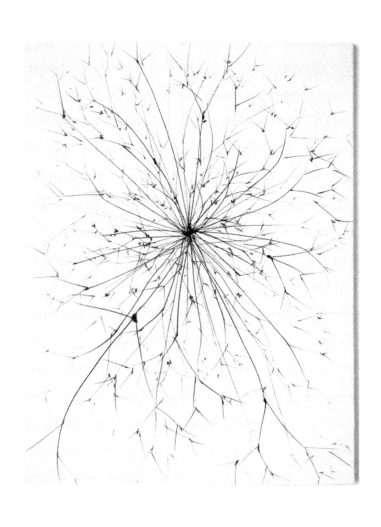

The man whose face the boy knew would hurt him

The boy raised his head from his pillow
    just enough
to see the man gleaming
    in the window.
It was an attic bedroom
    and the boy knew
no ladder would reach that high,
    but he knew also
that the man had a knife sharpened
    for one purpose only.
If the boy moved
    too suddenly
the man might move too.
    The boy kept his eyes closed
just enough so the man wouldn't
    suspect
the boy heard him breathing..
    Seventy years later and
he could still pick the man out of a crowd.
    The boy had never seen a face
that ravenous. Fleshy lips
    no meal could satisfy,
no kiss suffice. It was the mouth
    that would hurt him
the most, the boy was sure of this
    the way he was sure
of certain other things in his life:
    that he was neither brave
nor kind, nor helpful,
    nor good for much
except memorizing everything
    he'd ever done wrong,
every regret of his short life

though he knew,
even now, remembering
would not save him
from anyone or anything.

Matinee

Relatives were visiting from out of town
and since it was raining
and there's only so much you can say to cousins
you see every other year,
we all — even my father —
went to a movie about people wandering
in a jungle. Some were lost,

some were searching for them.
I only remember the cave,
and the naked women dancing in a circle.
I kept closing and opening my eyes
to make sure
I'd seen what I'd just seen.

The women on the screen had torches
they were dipping into the blaze
they leaped around
and around as if that's what fire demanded:
you must circle it,
you must join in the dance.
In the dark I could make out even darker places

between the women's legs
if I tried and I tried
not to. No one in my family seemed worried
or spoke afterwards
of what we'd witnessed.
I don't remember if those who were lost

were found. I did not dream those bodies
swaying and rising
as limber as if they were flames too.
I am as sure of this fact as I am
that at age eight on a rainy August day
in Hingham, Massachusetts
I watched women as old as the jungle

rise out of it
and feed a fire with an appetite
even greater than theirs.
They wanted something from me.
And I knew I would pay
for refusing.

Demeter

Before she hid me in fire's beating heart
she dipped her fingers in ambrosia
and breathed softly on me
the way you might on a flower
just before you pinch its stem.
Every night, she tucked me into the flames'
deepest arterial chambers
and watched
the way you might a coal burning so faithfully
you almost want to pluck it out
and thank it for its fervor,

Because I suffer, you must suffer,
my little fire–embossed foundling,
welcome distraction, trusty medallion,
Because nothing can ever flourish
long enough on the earth to console me.

Once you have held a scepter of fire in your fist,
once flames have been draped over your shoulders
how can you take anyone else's kiss?

Your mother's been dead for years.

Your mother's been dead for years.
She can't hurt you anymore.

You don't know my mother.

She's not at the window.
See, she's not listening on the stair.

.

As a child I knew never to underestimate her.

Look your mother has forgotten all about you
That's what the dead do. They forget.

You don't know my mother.

In Fifth Grade You Decide
You're an Alien

Though you do have bug eyes and a cowlick
that stands at attention like an antenna,
you doubt you're from somewhere as obvious as Mars
though sometimes you do
run your hand over your body
searching every opening for evidence,
that'll reveal you're not of the same planet
as are the kids who know how to breathe
through their noses
or hit a baseball instead of it hitting them
or laugh at the right moment.
There must be some proof
of why you are not like everyone else
if you just probe deep enough.
If you're an alien, it explains everything:
why at the lunch table you memorize
the distinctive way each boy chews,
the color of every girl's eyes,
how some kids have dimples and some don't,
valuable data perhaps
when you are called to account
for your time on earth
as surely you will be
when they return for you.
You don't know who they are
but you know they must be
coming for you.
Soon, you hope.

If You're Fifteen,
So Much Is Expected of You

Do you want to?
the girl asked.

                    Sure, the boy said
though he really didn't know
what she wished from him.
So he let her take his hand
And press it to her bosom.
Bosom.
What was he supposed to do now?
He did not let himself take too much pleasure.
He knew
what would come of that.

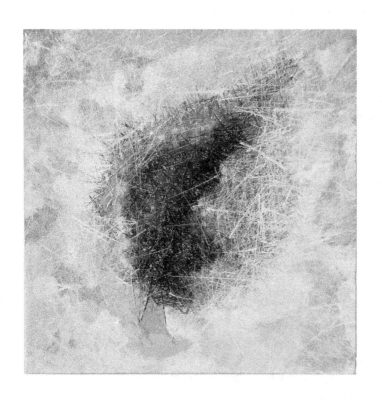

The Audition

What's your name?
the man asked.
The boy was waiting for his train.
All day at school
he'd been expected to perform tasks
he wasn't very good at.
So he enjoyed watching disheveled men
talk to their hands.
Policemen walked the aisles like ushers.
It was like being at the movies.
He even bought a snack he could make last
for the whole show.
Once a woman pulled a knife
on another old woman.
Once a man broke a bottle
over another man's head
The boy held each M&M in his mouth
as long as he could and then bit down.
What is your name?
the man repeated.
He kept sliding closer.
What are you studying?
The boy had his Latin open to Book 3
of Caesar's Punic Wars.
Read a little to me, the man said.
If the boy had learned anything
by the time he was fifteen,
it was that there are two types of people:
those meant for the movies,
those meant to sit in the dark
and watch the movie.
The boy knew he was the second type.
He lifted the man's hand off his lap.
He would stick to what he was good at.

C'est un secret

Lie down, the girl said.
      He had so many wounds
and she'd been searching for someone
      to heal.
But even with all his clothes off
      it was obvious
he was not going to be completely naked,
      he still had a secret
he could not reveal.
      Once a man had tried
to pry it out of him
      and might've if the boy had
known what the secret was
      he was carrying
so close to his breast he clutched it
      like a sealed document
someone had entrusted him with
      even if
he couldn't be sure who
      or when
or what they'd wanted from him.
      He read everyone's face.
His friend's father?
      His brother's roommate?
A man on the subway?
      A woman in the shadows?
A teacher staring at him
      across a lecture hall?
On a library table a book left open
      to a particular page?
A car slowing down,
      a window being rolled open
Are you the one meant
      to break the seal?
Or are you?

Hurt me

Hurt me
Kip used to whisper
to girls as soon as they were naked.
Only the girls never heard him.
Kip begged
and begged
but only in his head.

Hurt me
Kip said to the man in the toilet stall.
Wasn't that why they were there?
Hurt me
Hurt me
Hurt me
And then he fled.

A Boy's Hoarded Vocabulary

Never has a door the boy can shut
over and over

Say *closet* and he's naked inside coats
much too big for him.

Heavy is a hand on his bare shoulders,
Satin a river that touches every place on his body.

Say *cuffs* and he wakes up
next to a perfumed man.

Tu sais garder un secret?
On bad days he turns to thugs

that make no apologies
for what they might do:

grind, pound – one-syllabled fists
that put an end to things.

He's one of those boys who looks for a hiding place
as soon as he enters a room.

Sometimes two syllables are all it takes
to survive a doctor's office:

Meadow, fountain
His mouth's grateful. *Whistle* has its little gang

of consonants. *Licorice, halcyon, hologram,*
splatter, petulant, perdition.

How could a boy hate the world
if it had words like these?

Out

When I was seventeen
I came out
to my father.
It was 1961.
I sat in a chair.
My father sat in a chair.
It was dark
out. It was just as dark
inside.
The next day
he found me a doctor.
Come in,
the doctor said.
I was out.
I came in.

Jaden, François, Milos, Quentin, Pasqual

Passing me in the hall
how could they know what I'd dreamed up
for them, the night before
and the night before that?
The boys at school never suspected
the cruelties they were capable of
just because their parents had named them
                 Tristan or Simon, Sinjin or Rolf.
Each had his own tragic past
I invented for him, his own reason to hurt me:
a father who died while skydiving;
a mother locked in a place so far away
it might as well have been a castle;
a grandfather who liked to torture his grandchildren
to see what they'd do.
What happens to a kid like me?
Perhaps if he's lucky he grows up
and is smart enough to keep his thoughts
to himself. Maybe
he even finds a way to live in this world
while also living in another.
Or maybe he's foolish
and decides to trust words on the page
to keep his secrets.
Though, when have words ever been known
to keep anyone's secrets.

It Happened

You get a phone call
and then nothing's the same afterwards.

You turn on the news
and nothing's salvageable for this day and many days hereafter.

You ask a stranger how he is
and then he tells you.

You wander onto a website
and you can never un–see what you see.

You drive to your cousin's burnt house
and stare.

You place lilies of the valley on your mother's gravestone
even though you know the wind

will blow them off afterwards.
You sit next to your sister in the doctor's waiting room

and whisper *it'll be all right*
You make the mistake of waking up

the very morning you should've stayed in bed.
You answer the door

though the mailman's not in the habit of knocking
unless it's bad news.

The week after your friend has died
you dial her number.

You listen for her voice and know there's nothing you can do
to make time feel sorry for anyone.

The newspaper doesn't care
if it ruins your day.

The light falls on the words you are writing.
It offers no helpful suggestions

on how to get through this week
and the next.

DOG

For CWB, January, 31, 1968

Today I pick a window
to hold my son in.
He's just getting used to seeing
the world. I show him
a gull. *How did it get this far inland?*
I ask though he's hardly in a position
to know.
A woman on the street below
seems startled.
Is it the plane that's just shouldered its way
out of the clouds.
She looks as if she's about to start a fight
with someone. The sky?
A dog's watching her.
D O G I spell
as if it's never too early
to teach my boy
the truly important things
though right now he's not ready
to look at anything
besides his hands.
What a marvel: they open
and close.

May 4, 1970

My son's and my handmade
                    funnel thinking–caps
            almost pop off because
Isotope Feeney's up to his old tricks,
                    and every child's fate
            depends on us and Tom Terrific
and Mighty Manfred too –
                    only right then
            Manfred's pretending to be a rock
that wags its tail. *You're a genius, faithful*
                    Wonderdog.
            I'll turn into a boulder.
and block Isotope's laboratory door.
                    Dr. Isotope only momentarily
            gives up plotting
to take over the planet, world domination
                    proving a recurring motif
            on *Captain Kangaroo,*
Curses, now I can't even lace
                    every kid's Froot Loops
            with my secret amnesia formula?
What do you do, face–to–face with evil
                    five days a week
            especially if you're three
and thirty and there seems to be no end
                    to villains:
            Captain Destructo, Radiation Man,
Sweet Tooth Sam, Crabby Appleton?
                    Who knows what mischief
            a day will bring?
Featherduster? Flea? Golden key.
                    I can be anything you see.
            How I do it puzzles even me.

Yet another morning we help Tom Terrific
               turn into what he must
     to save the world
but to do so we must close our eyes
              and once again think
     hard. Very hard.

How We Get Through a Day
For R, L, and V intrepid souls

1 – if you're ten

I hate museums.
               You can't make me go,
          she holds fast to the kitchen counter
as if afraid her grandmother's going to
               drag her
          out of the house.
Leave me alone, she says
               to her Noono
          who's brought her cocoa.
All of a sudden, she despises cocoa.
               She doesn't know why
          her father packed all his tools,
only that she wasn't there
               when he left with them
          and she should have been.

2 – if you're fourteen,

Her sister's tired, morning, noon,
               and night: too worn out
          to think of anything
but her unfinished math homework.
               Soccer, school newspaper,
          swim team, theater club.
she's too exhausted now
               even to yell
          at her ten–year–old sister
sobbing so determinedly
               in the next room
          what's a big sister to do
but get out of bed and say everything
               will be all right,
          though she knows
it will never be right again.

3 – if you're forty-seven,

Their mother, home from the office,
                    the cleaners,
          the library, the drugstore,
makes SpaghettiOs
                    the one meal
          they all can count on
liking. After swim practice,
                    she works out the tangles
                of one daughter's hair
          and then another's.
They stay as still as possible.
                    Even if it hurts
          they say
it doesn't hurt.

What I Did the Morning Before
I Hit a Man on His Bicycle

Brought in my trash barrels.

Brought in my neighbor's trash barrels.

Brought in the newspaper: in other words, carried in shootings
   and train wrecks and molesting priests.

Ate the same breakfast I ate the day before: a frozen waffle.

Took my six morning pills: the hard to swallow one first.

Read a little: about the landscape painter Inness who scored
   deep gouges in the sky.

Wrote a check for a scholarship in the name of a colleague
   with whom I'd quarreled for years.

Fed the cats: tried to insure an equal distribution of wealth.

Got in the car and backed out of my driveway

It wasn't raining but birds had decorated the windshield.

   so I put on the wipers

Couldn't see the man on the bicycle: tapped the bike so lightly
he didn't even fall off

Stopped the car: begged his forgiveness and he gave it, straddling his
bike

   the way bicyclists do

Got out of my car and inspected his bike.

Begged his forgiveness again

And again: not only had he almost been killed by me
   but now he had to comfort me.

Got back in my car

Watched his bike as it crested the hill.

Drove as slowly as I could, even though the car clearly wanted to go
faster.

Turned right: though I was supposed to go left

Pulled over to the side of the road: saw the man still flying
   into the air, light as a leaf.

Handcuffs

The handcuffs aren't that tight
though the cops tried
to make them tight enough
perhaps so the bruises would help me
remember being dragged
across the pavement by something as banal
as plastic. If they'd been metal
I might have clung to a little dignity.
But to be bound in black plastic
that could've come from Walmart?
Is this what we revolutionaries get reduced to?
Not saving the planet
but crammed with thirty people
into a van that holds twenty,
all the while worrying about having to take a leak.
What was I thinking?
That if I lay down on a rainy street
the world might become a slightly better place?
Protect the planet?
I can't even summon the right words to comfort my grandkids
when they sulk home from school.
I can't even assure my wife
that this is not going to be one of those days
I stare out the window
and long for another world
to live in all the while trying to
make the best of living in this one.

What Did I Do With It?

Though my mother wasn't in handcuffs
the man tilted down her head anyway
just as I'd seen cops do
in movies, nudging a suspect into a patrol car.

After that I slept with my arms crossed
so tightly you'd have thought
I was protecting some treasure
that any minute might be ripped from me.

When I grew old enough to vanish
and ride the city buses
men slipped their hands into my pockets.
Searching for what?

Some days in the middle of a poem we're discussing
I'll look down at my students
and they'll look up at me
as if I had something they needed

if only I knew how to give it to them.
Some days I gaze at my grandson
Maybe now I'll finally tell him what I've been waiting
till he was old enough

to tell him. But then I turn away.
The way I turned away
when my father stared at me as if it was up to me
to make things right.

When my friend pressed against me
as if I was holding on to the very thing
that could save him
I turned away. I turned also from my wife

when I could have turned and said
This is what I have to offer. Take it.
But what is it
I clutch still so tightly I can't part with it

though I know too well that years ago I let it
be taken from me?

Morrisville Community Town Park

Behind us, boys are fighting
                    for their lives
        in the last of the seventh,
the Braves against the Yankees, the grass
                    that yellow

        green
baseball fields become under lights
                    and my grandson and I
        keep glancing back
at the game over our shoulders
                    when we aren't
        counting Winchesters
and Colt 45s. Want to look at more guns
                    than you ever have?
        Come to an Anti-Gun rally,
even the names make you want
                    to own them: Nighthawk,
        and Shadow Op, Marlin,
and Custom Sako Finnwolf
                    dark rivered grain
        any woodworker would admire.
My grandson has just learned to count
                    and he counts

        up to 54
guns and 26 names of children
                    Madeline Hsu,
        Chase Kowalski, Noah Pozner.
Charlotte Bacon, Daniel Barden, Rachel Davino,
                    Olivia Engel…
        Caroline Previdi,
Avielle Richman, Benjamin Wheeler.
                    The names hover
        after they're spoken.
It's that time of day you hear birds
                    but can't see them.
        By dusk

even the women with rifles
                    slung over their backs
        have grown tired
of the explosions they detonate
        with their voices
Hey pussy, you're next!
                    a man shouts
        halfheartedly at me.
Don't ask, I tell four-year-old Tyler –
                    *I'll explain
        later.* Apparently
the Braves have blown their lead
                    across the park
        and we can see heads bowed
and parents trying
                    what parents have always tried:
        to make a bad thing
bearable. *Climb in the car,*
                    I say to my grandson.
        How about some ice cream?

The Day Before Surgery

Here is Vienna. Here is where a man turned to music
when all else failed. D. Weiss

Tomorrow
my skin will be peeled back
just below my collar bone.
and a little machine lifted out of me
to see if it's up to the task
                              asked of it,
but at this moment no one is checking the wires
to my heart, Sorry,
knife, you'll get your chance
in a few hours
                              Right now, in class,
a t–shirted boy is raising his hand
to ask if Vienna is in Germany
and I can see the rivers
on the inside of his arm.
It's hard for me to go on teaching
if kids insist on being naked
                              beneath their clothes.
                    Inside my chest,
an unrepentant worm,
its ferocious mandibles
                    gnaw
on everything I feed it.
Was it already uncoiling as I hid in the womb?
Is it my fault I let it feast
on my heart?

I Remember

I remember the night sky
my mother offered me to,
I remember the knife in her hand.

I remember the girl who, when I was fifteen,
loved me as mercilessly
as the sea loves the land.

I remember my father, naked, standing over me
so close to my bed
I could have reached out and cupped
what I thought to be the secret of life.

I remember a stranger who insisted
that I undress in front of him
if I wanted to understand poetry.

I remember wrapping my arms around myself.

I remember opening a book
as if it was the only door in the house
I could shut behind me.

Why the seventy-five year-old man holds matches to his ankles

Because he's burned too many other incriminating places on his body.
Because his shoulders and belly are already covered

with dot–to–dot puzzles.
Because, if he had a sense of humor and a permanent marker, he'd count

how many different animals he could make appear
out of the scars up and down his legs.

Because he has no sense of humor, but plenty of matches.
Because he hides them

in his gym bag, his briefcase, behind his grandson's
school picture, in the bottom of his junk drawer,

Because if he doesn't burn himself, he'll combust.
Though he knows men don't explode

simply because they're disappointments to long–dead fathers
or long–suffering wives.

Because he can't afford to kill himself right now; because he has to
pick up his granddaughter at field hockey.

Because suicide – *sui, of oneself, and cidium, n. 2nd declension* –
sounds imposingly Latinate,

requiring too much self–confidence and self–importance –
because it's so much less trouble

to hold a match to your ankles
till you're begging for mercy from a flame.

Because flames, in certain circumstances, do find it in themselves
to grant mercy.

Where Do I Fall on the Spectrum?

See that kid riding his half–pipe next–door?
I wouldn't mind getting so close to him
I could taste the salt on his shoulders.

But I am not about to
make love to a fifteen–year–old boy any more than I'm likely to
have sex with a rufous–throated nuthatch

just landed on my windowsill.
All afternoon
the boy propels himself off the driveway

as if that's what a kid is supposed to
alone on a Saturday.
The black–capped bird pays no attention to him

nor to the man
just inside the window's curtains
watching.

Today the eyes get to decide
what's important
and what's important today

is a boy turned glistening
by his own sweat
and a blue–grey bird

that's just noticed itself
in the glass.
I am right behind the curtains.

I am one of those
who keep a window between him
and everything he longs for.

There must be a name
for such a man,
for such longings. Look it up.

I Was Wrong

As a boy I kept wishing
                         when I woke up
             I'd be different.
Maybe sleep would've turned me
                   strong
          or brave
and I'd not need to be ashamed
                    anymore
          of having a body
that smelled like mildewed bread
                  or a mind
          greedier
than a cockroach. How could I
                 expect
          to do anything of worth
with such spindly legs and
                   gluttonous eyes?
          I kept hoping
I'd finally get old
                 enough
          to be done
with wanting things
                   I had no right
          to want.
I was wrong.

What Do You After a
Friend Has Killed Herself?

I'm finally with the butterflies. Thousands
of them. I refuse to believe otherwise and
I hope you believe that too. In that lies our only health.

First, I punish Thelonious Monk, Miles Davis, Django Reinhardt,
Janis Joplin, Martha and the Vandals, Fats Domino,
and a thousand or so other musicians
whose CDs my friend had arranged not by name but aura.
If they couldn't save a soul like Sandy, what good were they?
Banished to trashbags now, they'll get no second chances.

Every single window plant that failed to make air
worth breathing I don't just dump, I rip out
of the only domicile it has known: wounded begonia, tulips
in their glass dome, a Buddha's bellyful of irises,
even flighty amaryllis insisting till the very end
on showing off. I flush the pot stash I just uncovered; medicinal,

recreational — who cares now? Every single pill
must pay. Tylenol, Aleve, Motrin. It isn't enough
to dispose of them. In the mortar and pestle dug out of the closet
I pound into oblivion: astragalus root, hops,
chelated zinc, valerian, liothyronine, lysin,
levothyroxine, lithium, so many good intentions

beginning with l. What use now are Ram Das
and Deepak Chopra, Joseph Campbell and James Hillman,
Eckhart Tolle and the Dali Lama, Lau Tzu
and the I Ching, Shiva and Sappho, Cybele and Susanne Langer,
Vievee Frances and Martha Rhodes. Yes,
my friend would've wished me to find homes for her books,

especially all those thin poetry volumes
with their generous inscriptions, but I commit them all
now to flames, a whole shelf of Mark Doty and Louise Glück

gone up in smoke. Beauty gets no last words.
No one gets to open Wisława Syzmborska
or Naomi Sahib Nye and think, "Ah, Sandy read these pages!"

Out to the curb go even the Mondays–with–Marie poets,
Kumar, McKee, McBride, Steginsky, Fanok, Rivers,
Holloway, Wrezniewski, Nolan.. I shred all those
be brave, don't forget we love you cards
we sent. The pillows that refused to give my friend comfort
when comfort was needed. The china from her first marriage,

the porcelain puppets from her second.
Hear that sound? That's everything fragile
breaking. Even the bamboo chest with its spare bullets,
and firearm registration. Dearest, that fringed
butterfly you loved so much you let it hover over your bed?
I broke the glass. I sent it on its way.

The seventy-five-year-old grandfather is not worried about death anymore.

If he's dead, that's the end
of fretting over
whether Tyler makes the high school J.V.,
or
Josie finds someone lucky enough to love her as we
                   all love her
or
Zack decides to let the world see how amazing he is
or
Jake finds a job that'll keep him from growing restless
or
Maggie realizes that life's not so bad, even if it continually disap-
points her
or
Sadie lets herself remember how much fun it was being four.
Henceforth, also
                 this old man will not be responsible for ending
world hunger, global warming,
If I'm dead,
then all my worries are over,
He says over and over
but only in his head.

As She Knew She Must

Why try to imagine the conclusive minutes
in my friend's life, her index finger
introducing itself to the ready—to—be—of—service
trigger; the neurotransmitters, those obliging
servants bustling about their business
following last minute instructions
of the mistress of the house;
the amygdala deciding now
better than later, here
rather than there, under this tulip tree
near that trout lily
right after letting the brain have one final look
at an osprey: time
to do what she'd been putting off
perhaps all her life?
Don't go, I had said into the phone.
Don't, whatever it costs you, go.
And then a day later she went.
As she knew she must.

Opa Bequeaths His Imaginary Friends to His Grandchildren

To my oldest granddaughter, Josephine,
I leave Wobbly.
He needs someone who won't think less of him
for being afraid. Josie knows how he frets.
     He's always been scared of even more than I have.

To my oldest grandsons, Jake and Zack,
I leave Round Fat Mr. Prune.
When they were four and three, they flew everywhere with him
in a rocketship Zack gave a drill
so it could spin through the earth's crust.
Even at the earth's fiery core lives needed saving.

To Maggie and her best friend Arianna I leave Oliver.
I'd be frantic, looking for him.
and *Oh, Opa*, the girls would say, *Come closer
to the pool* and, wouldn't you know it, there'd be Oliver
and Maggie and Arianna, ready to splash me
till I had no choice but to jump in the water too.

To Sadie and her best friend Annalise
I leave the imaginary friends Sadie invented at three
and then at four sent to China.
She told me, one morning, with a smile
they were dead. A month later
she said that Tootie, Coco, and Fuzzball were in Paris
but still dead.

To Tyler I leave the Calachiis
and Xochimilko No one knows better than Tyler
how to keep winged assassins
and archvillains from wreaking more havoc on the world
than the world can handle.
Long Arms, Dr. Ice, and Randy Savage?
They can still prove of immeasurable help.

Because all six of my grandchildren had imaginary friends
I made up Wobbly
and he was lonely and so he made up Oliver
and Oliver got jealous and made up his own imaginary friend:
Nobody. Where I am going I can take Nobody
He won't be you, my irreplaceable ones,
but he'll be good company.

A Boy Knocks At My Door

A boy knocks at my door,
and, yes, he has wings,
though I can barely make them out
under his sweatshirt.
He's one of those kids
who always look naked.
even when fully dressed
No, he is not the Angel of Death,
but, yes, he announces
he has come to offer me absolution,
and so I kneel before him
and he places his hand lightly
on my head –
with just enough pressure so I know
he means it.
It's as simple as that.

Till Death Do Us Part

Who led you off to bed when you were eleven
and tugged off your shirt
and lay down beside you
and kissed the sweet spot under your arms,
your belly? Who turned you over
and placed his mouth on the small of your back,
and gave you something else to think about
besides how hopelessly stupid
how inconsiderate, how ugly you were.

When you were seventeen
who rode the bus with you after football games,
who kept your eyes scanning the seats
for the nape of a wide receiver's neck,
a pimply boy's shirtless arms, those glistening hairs?

Who will find your bed in the nursing home,
and, despite all the tubing,
manage to hold you in his arms
after your family has finally left
tired of trying to think of what to say to you?
Who will give you something else to consider
besides what the doctors had said?
Who will seek out the hollows of your knees,
the heels of your feet
as if every part of you still deserves to be comforted?

Leif, Rafe. Rafe, Leif

How do I explain the boy I've just made up
now that I'm seventy-five

to the boy I made up when I was fifteen
and needed someone to adore

because life didn't seem worth the effort
unless I had something to die for

and I knew nothing better to die for
than a boy I gave wings

so he could test his bright ambitions
and then I had to let him slip away.

Now far closer to death now than I was
at fifteen to being born,

I call upon another boy
one just as in need of wings.
.

He is the patient, but resolute angel
that will carry me through that last sleep

into which I refuse to go
alone.

This Time It's My Window

This time, it's my window
someone's knocking at and so quietly
he could be mistaken for a sycamore branch
or honey locust that's suddenly decided
it had business with me
and only me

Of course, I answer, but it's not whom I expected
but a man as weather-beaten
as the trees
assigned the task of guarding my house.
Have you come to set me free?
I'm used to be being facetious

with trees. That seems my prerogative
having grown almost as ancient
as they are. This man appears even older.
So I invite him in,
but *no*, he says,
as if I've just been guilty of a breach of manners

What can I do for you?
I inquire. I decide to be as deferential to him
as I would to a tree.
No, he says. *It's rather what I can do for you.*
And to my surprise
he kisses me

on the cheek as lightly as I remember kissing girls
I didn't wish to scare off.
And then he turns
and walks away with the measured gait
of someone who's accomplished exactly
what he came to do

and now has other obligations.
That's how the light falling through trees finds you
sometimes and then
it heads off to where, in the first place, it had meant to go
though you remember its touch
long after it seems reasonable to do so.

What if, the boy had nowhere to go for absolution?

What if at the end of a road
the boy hadn't realized was there till he turned onto it

a house introduced itself,
and what if the boy had knocked softly at the door

and a man opened it
and led the boy into a windowed room empty of everything

but light
and in that light the man slipped each of the boy's shirt buttons

out of his shirt's little hollow embraces
and what if the boy lifted his arms

as if he'd been training for this all his short life:
to whirl and spin across the floor

using every muscle of his nine–year–old body.
What if this was what the boy had come for?

More would be demanded of him.
The boy knew this, but for now

he flickered,
a firefly set loose

in a glass dome. And I?
What if I too had danced for my father?

Forgive me.

What some of us say
the moment we wake up.

Not talking to anyone
in particular.

We know the light in the window has no interest
in forgiving anyone.

It has other pressing obligations.
Pardon me,

A man says
as he opens his eyes.

And the light does.
It didn't intend to,

but it does.

Collected Poems

No matter what door
you open

it is always to the same room.
You thought it might lead

to a different room.
But, no, it's the same room.

Go in.
You are expected there.

Acknowledgments

This book would not have been possible without the guidance of poet Ethel Rackin, the wise counsel of Anne Tax and Jim Fillman, the friendship of Helen Lawton Wilson, the inspiration of Pam and Herb Perkins–Frederick, and the love of Mary Ann Bursk.

With gratitude to *River Heron* where "Why a Seventy–Five Year Old Man Holds Matches to his Ankles" appeared first.

With gratitude to the painter Danielle Bursk whose art continues to invite us to explore life's ineluctable and often delectable mysteries.

With gratitude to Samantha Atzeni and Adam Wilson and all the *Read Furiously* committed and valiant team.

A Note to Our Furious Readers

From all of us at Read Furiously, we hope you enjoyed our latest poetry collection, *Dear Terror*.

There are countless narratives in this world and we would like to share as many of them as possible with our Furious Readers.

It is with this in mind that we pledge to donate a portion of these book sales to causes that are special to Read Furiously and the creators involved in *Dear Terror*. These causes are chosen with the intent to better the lives of others who are struggling to tell their own stories.

Reading is more than a passive activity – it is the opportunity to play an active role within our world. At Read Furiously, its editors and its creators wish to add an active voice to the world we all share because we believe any growth within the company is aimless if we can't also nurture positive changes in our local and global communities. The causes we support are not politically driven, but are culturally and socially–based to encourage a sense of civic responsibility associated with the act of reading. Each cause has been researched thoroughly, discussed openly, and voted upon carefully by our team of Read Furiously editors.

To find out more about who, what, why, and where Read Furiously lends its support, please visit our website at readfuriously.com/charity

Happy reading and giving, Furious Readers!

Read Often, Read Well,
Read Furiously!